LEARNING ADVENTURES
IN MATH
Grades 3-4

By the Staff of Score@Kaplan

Foreword by Alan Tripp

Simon & Schuster

This series is dedicated to our Score@Kaplan parents and children—thank you for making these books possible.

Published by
Kaplan Educational Centers and Simon & Schuster
1230 Avenue of the Americas
New York, NY 10020

Copyright © 1998 by Kaplan Educational Centers

All rights reserved. No part of this book may be reproduced or transmitted in any form or by any means, electronic or mechanical, including photocopying, recording, or by any information storage and retrieval system, without the written permission of the Publisher, except where permitted by law.

Kaplan is a registered trademark of Kaplan Educational Centers.

Special thanks to: Elissa Grayer, Doreen Beauregard, Julie Schmidt, Rebecca Geller Schwartz, Linda Lott, Janet Cassidy, Marlene Greil, Nancy McDonald, Sarah Jane Bryan, Chris Wilsdon, Janet Montal, Jeannette Sanderson, David Stienecker, Dan Greenberg, Kathy Wilmore, Dorrie Berkowitz, and Molly Walsh

Head Coach and General Manager, Score@Kaplan: Alan Tripp
President, Score@Kaplan: Robert L. Waldron
Series Content and Development: Mega-Books
Project Editor: Mary Pearce
Production Editor: Donna Mackay, Graphic Circle Inc.
Art Director: Elana Goren-Totino
Illustrators: Rick Brown, Ryan Brown, Sandy Forrest, Larry Nolte, Evan Polenghi, Fred Schrier, Peter Spacek, Arnie Ten
Cover Design: Cheung Tai
Cover Photograph: Michael Britto

Manufactured in the United States of America
Published Simultaneously in Canada

March 1998
10 9 8 7 6 5 4 3 2 1

ISBN:0-684-84432-X

Contents

Grade Three

Grade Four

Dear Parents,

Your child's success in school is important to you, and at Score@Kaplan we are always pleased when the kids who attend our educational centers do well on their report cards. But what we really want for our kids is not just good grades. We also want everything that good grades are supposed to represent:

- We want our kids to master the key communication systems that make civilization possible: language (spoken and written), math, the visual arts, and music.
- We want them to build their critical-thinking skills so they can understand, appreciate, and improve their world.
- We want them to continually increase their knowledge and to value learning as the key to a happy, successful life.
- We want them to always do their best, to persist when challenged, to be a force for good, and to help others whenever they can.

These are ambitious goals, but our children deserve no less. We at Score@Kaplan have already helped thousands of children across the country in our centers, and we hope this series of books for children in first through sixth grades will reach many more households.

Simple Principles

We owe the remarkable success of Score@Kaplan to a few simple principles. This book was developed with these principles in mind.

- We expect every child to succeed.
- We make it possible for every child to succeed.
- We reinforce every instance of success, no matter how small.

Assessing Your Child

One helpful approach in assessing your child's skills is to ask yourself the following questions.

- How much is my child reading? At what level of difficulty?
- Has my child mastered appropriate language arts skills, such as spelling, grammar, and syntax?
- Does my child have the ability to express appropriately complex thoughts when speaking or writing?
- Does my child demonstrate mastery of all age-appropriate math skills, such as mastery of addition and subtraction facts, multiplication tables, division rules, and so on?

These questions are a good starting place and may give you new insights into your child's academic situation.

What's Going on at School

Parents will always need to monitor the situation at school and take responsibility for their child's learning. You should find out what your child should be learning at each grade level and match that against what your child actually learns.

The activity pages in *Learning Adventures* were developed using the standards developed by the professional teachers associations. As your child explores the activities in *Learning Adventures*, you might find that a particular concept hasn't been taught in school or hasn't yet been mastered by your child. This presents a great opportunity for both of you. Together you can learn something new.

Encouraging Your Child to Learn at Home

This book is full of fun learning activities you can do with your child to build understanding of key concepts in language arts, math, and science. Most activities are designed for your child to do independently. But, that doesn't mean that you can't work on them together or invite your child to share the work with you. As you help your child learn, please bear in mind the following observations drawn from experience in our centers:

- Positive reinforcement is the key. Try to maintain a ratio of at least five positive remarks to every negative one.
- All praise must be genuine. Try praises such as: "That was a good try," "You got this part of it right," or "I'm proud of you for doing your best, even though it was hard."
- When a child gets stuck, giving the answer is often not the most efficient way to help. Ask open-ended questions, or rephrase the problem.
- Remember to be patient and supportive. Children need to learn that hard work pays off.

There's More to Life Than Academic Learning

Most parents recognize that academic excellence is just one of the many things they would like to ensure for their children. At Score@Kaplan, we are committed to developing the whole child. These books are designed to emphasize academic skills and critical thinking, as well as provide an opportunity for positive reinforcement and encouragement from you, the parent.

We wish you a successful and rewarding experience as you and your child embark upon this learning adventure together.

Alan Tripp
General Manager
Score@Kaplan

Dear Kids,

Get your pencils sharpened and put your game face on! You're about to start a Learning Adventure. This book is filled with puzzles, games, riddles and lots of other fun stuff. You can do them alone or with your family and friends. While you're at it, you'll exercise your brain.

If you get stuck on something, look for the Score coaches. Think of them as your personal brain trainers. You can also check your answers on pages 65-70, if you really have to.

We know you will do a great job. That's why we have a special puzzle inside. After you do three or four pages, you'll see a puzzle piece. Cut it out, then glue it or tape it in place on page 64. When you're done with the book, the puzzle will be done, too. Then you'll find a secret message from us.

So, pump up your mind muscles and get ready to Score. You'll have a blast and boost your brain power at the same time.

Go for it!

Your Coaches at Score

NAME

Dog-Tired Numbers

It's bedtime at Rover Ranch, where every dog is named
after a number. Read the number on each bed. Write it
in numerals on the line. Then find the pooch with the
same number. Draw a line connecting each pup to his
own bed.

One thousand, two hundred eight

Six thousand, four hundred ten

Three thousand, seven hundred

Four thousand, one hundred sixty

Three thousand, seven

One thousand, twenty-eight

1,028   3,700   3,007   6,410   1,208   4,160

Remember the place
value of each number.
For example:

5,208

Thousands · Tens · Ones
Hundreds

Around the House: See what 1,000 really means.
Ask a grown-up's permission, and then try counting out 1,000
pieces of breakfast cereal. Are there 1,000 pieces in a box?
How much space does 1,000 pieces take up?

NAME _____

Lots of Letters!

Help Mail Carrier Marvin deliver these letters! The addresses are written in words. Write each one in numbers in the blanks. Then find a house with the same number. Write the name of the person who lives there in the second blank. We did one for you.

Remember what each place stands for.

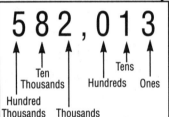

582,013

↑ Hundred Thousands
↑ Ten Thousands
↑ Thousands
↑ Hundreds
↑ Tens
↑ Ones

A.

Seven hundred forty-two thousand, two hundred eighty

House number: __742,280__

Deliver to: __Perry Meter__

B.

Two hundred thirty thousand, seven hundred four

House number: _____

Deliver to: _____

C.

Twenty-three thousand, seventy four

House number: _____

Deliver to: _____

D.

Seven hundred four thousand, two hundred eight

House number: _____

Deliver to: _____

Cal Q. Later
23,074

Dee Nominator
704,208

Perry Meter
742,280

Mel T. Plication
230,704

2

Grade 3

NAME_____

Turtle Triathlon

Tommy, Tammy, and Timmy Turtle just competed in the
Turtle Triathlon. Each race was slow but steady. They are
turtles, after all! Whoever placed first in 2 out of the 3
races is the winner. Put their race times in order to find
the winner. We started one for you.

1. Here are the finishing times for the running race.

Tommy: 2,468 minutes_____

Tammy: 1,985 minutes_____first place_____

Timmy: 2,811 minutes_____

2. Here are the finishing times for the swimming race.

Tommy: 8,361 minutes_____

Tammy: 8,631 minutes_____

Timmy: 6,894 minutes_____

3. Here are the finishing times for the bike race.

Tommy: 4,760 minutes_____

Tammy: 4,507 minutes_____

Timmy: 5,300 minutes_____

Remember,
whoever finishes
a race in the
fewest number
of minutes wins.

Bonus: Who won the Turtle Triathlon?_____

Around the House: Use a school directory or telephone
book to find the last 4 digits in the phone numbers of friends.
Write these 4-digit numbers. Then put them in order from least
to greatest.

NAME _____

Zelda's Expanding Zoo

Zookeeper Zelda wants people to learn something when they visit her zoo. Here are some questions she asks visitors. Each question is followed by a number in expanded form. Before each answer, there is a number in standard form. Match the expanded form with the standard form to find the answer to each question. Circle your answers. The first one is done for you.

> Remember, a number in *standard* form looks like this:
> 2,473
> A number in *expanded* form looks like this:
> 2,000 + 400 + 70 + 3

> Terrific job! Cut out the puzzle piece. Glue or tape it in place on page 64.

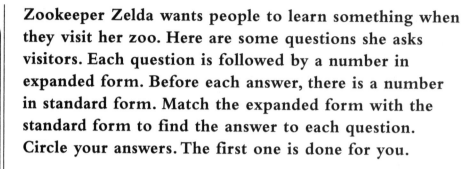

1. What is the fastest mammal?   (80 + 4)
   (804) Horse   (84) Cheetah   (48) Antelope

2. What is the heaviest land animal?   (300 + 50 + 7)
   (357) African elephant (30,057) Hippopotamus
   (3,507) Rhinoceros

3. What is the largest bird? (4,000 + 20 + 6)
   (4,026) Ostrich   (426) Stork   (4,206) Emperor penguin

4. What is the longest snake? (100 + 90 + 4)
   (1,904) King cobra   (1,094) Anaconda
   (194) Reticulated python

5. Besides the human being, what is the smartest mammal?
   (7,000 + 20)
   (7,020) Chimpanzee   (720) Dolphin   (7,002) Orangutan

6. Which animal sleeps the most hours each day?
   (2,000 + 800 + 10 + 8)
   (2,808) Cat   (2,818) Koala   (288) Sloth

Around the House: Use a reference book to find an interesting animal fact. Write a question and answer choices as above. Then let a family member figure out the answer.

NAME_____

Count on Sports

Read about each athlete. Then look at the numbers below. Each athlete started counting. Fill in the missing numbers in the counting pattern. Then write the name of the person who is talking.

Mi Won likes to play basketball. She counts her baskets by 2s.

Paul likes to swim. He counts his strokes by 10s.

Diana likes to play soccer. She counts her goals by 5s.

5, 10, 15, ____ , ____ , ____ ,
____ , ____ , ____ , ____

1. Who is counting?

_____

2, 4, 6, 8, 10, 12, ____ ,
____ , ____ , ____ , ____ , ____ ,
____ , ____ , ____ , ____ , ____

2. Who is counting?

_____

10, 20, ____ , ____ , ____

3. Who is counting?

_____

Around the House: Count on around the house. How many socks do you have? Count them by 2s. How many books do you have? Count them by 5s. What can you count by 10s? How many do you have?

NAME _____

Western Round-Up

Sidesaddle Sally sold five items in her western store today. Round each price to the nearest ten or hundred. One is done for you. Then use your rounded prices to find out who bought what.

To round to
the nearest ten,
round up if the
ones place is
5 or greater.
Otherwise, round
down.

To round to the
nearest hundred,
round up if the
tens place is
5 or greater.
Otherwise, round
down.

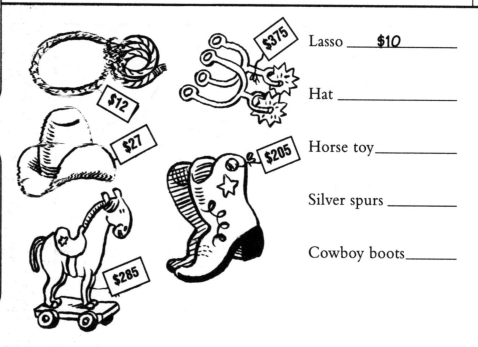

Lasso _____ **$10** _____

Hat _____

Horse toy _____

Silver spurs _____

Cowboy boots _____

1. Mel spent about $400. Which item did he buy? _____
2. Liza spent about $10. Which item did she buy? _____
3. Juanita spent about $200. Which item did she buy? _____
4. Bob spent about $30. Which item did he buy? _____
5. Leann spent about $300. Which item did she buy? _____

Around the House: Look in a newspaper or magazine for advertised prices of clothes. Round them to the nearest ten. Then look for prices of items like TVs and computers. Round to the nearest hundred. How do you think rounding might come in handy when you are shopping?

NAME_____

Spinning Thousands

Have you ever played a game that took 9,000 points to win? This game does, but don't worry—it's easy. Ask a friend or family member to play the game with you. Here's how:

1. On your first turn, spin the spinner, and then write the number you land on at the top of the work space.
2. On your next turn, add the number you land on to the number you wrote in the work space to get a total.
3. On your other turns, keep adding the numbers you land on to get a new total.
4. The first player whose total is over 9,000 wins.

MAKE A SPINNER
Put a pencil point through the end of a paper clip at the center of the spinner. Hold the pencil straight up while you spin the clip.

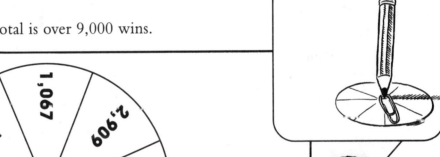

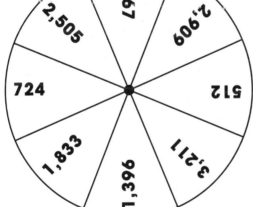

Work Space

Player Name_____	Player Name_____

NAME _____

Subtraction Tic-Tac-Toe

Practice your subtraction skills with Subtraction Tic-Tac-Toe. The object of the game is to get 4 Xs in a row—across, down, or diagonally! Here's how to play.

1. Pick 2 numbers from the Number Box. Subtract the smaller number from the larger number. (Remember: the larger number goes on top.)
2. Make an "X" over your answer on the board.
3. Keep going until you have 4 in a row.

When you subtract, you have to *regroup,* or borrow, if a digit in the top number is smaller than a digit in the bottom number.

You did it! Now you can cut out the puzzle piece. Figure out where it goes in the puzzle frame on page 64.

Number Box

2,021	824
1,103	556
912	79

Answer Board

191	1,465	268	918
833	FREE	1,942	279
1,109	88	477	1,024
547	745	1,197	356

Around the House: Write down the year you were born and the year an adult was born. Try to guess the difference in your ages. Then do the math. How close was your guess?

NAME

Hop, Hop, Hooray!

Help Horace the frog hop to dry land! As he hops from lily pad to lily pad, he must stop to solve multiplication problems. When you get to each problem, write in a number to solve the problem. Then look at the number you wrote. If the pad says "hop up," move forward that many spaces. If the pad says "hop back," move backward that many spaces. Horace did the first one for you.

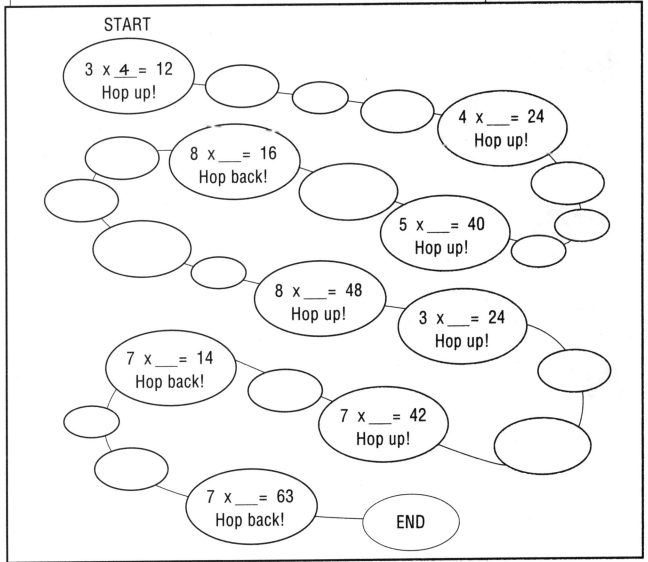

START

3 x __4__ = 12
Hop up!

4 x ___ = 24
Hop up!

8 x ___ = 16
Hop back!

5 x ___ = 40
Hop up!

8 x ___ = 48
Hop up!

3 x ___ = 24
Hop up!

7 x ___ = 14
Hop back!

7 x ___ = 42
Hop up!

7 x ___ = 63
Hop back!

END

NAME _____

Multiplying Flies

The flies in the pond were glad that Horace the Frog was busy hopping around. He was too busy to eat any of them! Three flies phoned fly friends and invited them to visit. Do the multiplication in each bubble. The answer shows how many friends each fly invited.

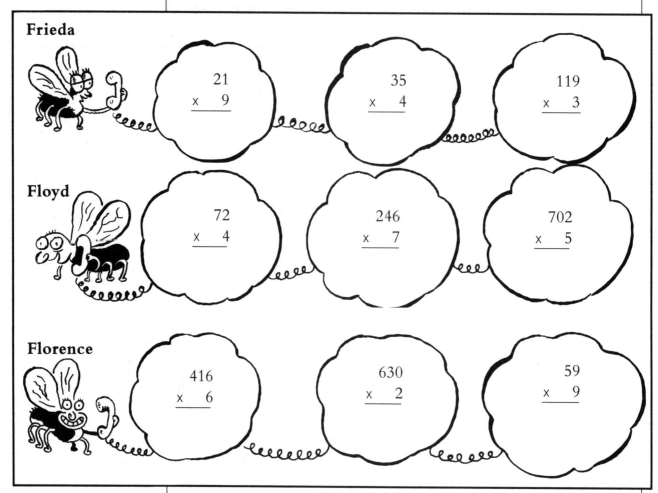

Frieda

$$\begin{array}{r} 21 \\ \times\ \ 9 \\ \hline \end{array}$$

$$\begin{array}{r} 35 \\ \times\ \ 4 \\ \hline \end{array}$$

$$\begin{array}{r} 119 \\ \times\ \ \ 3 \\ \hline \end{array}$$

Floyd

$$\begin{array}{r} 72 \\ \times\ \ 4 \\ \hline \end{array}$$

$$\begin{array}{r} 246 \\ \times\ \ \ 7 \\ \hline \end{array}$$

$$\begin{array}{r} 702 \\ \times\ \ \ 5 \\ \hline \end{array}$$

Florence

$$\begin{array}{r} 416 \\ \times\ \ \ 6 \\ \hline \end{array}$$

$$\begin{array}{r} 630 \\ \times\ \ \ 2 \\ \hline \end{array}$$

$$\begin{array}{r} 59 \\ \times\ \ 9 \\ \hline \end{array}$$

Check Yourself: Who invited the most friends? Add together your answers for each fly's calls. Floyd should have invited the most, followed by Florence, and then Frieda. If this doesn't match your answers, go back and check your computation.

NAME _____

Bloog Adventures!

In this game, you help a friendly Martian named Bloog collect asteroids. Your job is to find the path that gives you the highest score. Here's how to play:

1. Solve the problem in the circle labeled START. Write your answer on the line. That's the number of asteroids you start with.
2. Move in any direction, but don't pass a circle more than once.
3. At each circle, you collect more asteroids. To find out how many, multiply the numbers and write the answer on the line. Add those asteroids to the amount you already have.
4. To win, you must find the path that gives you the highest number of asteroids and gets you to FINISH in 5 moves.

Work in pencil so you can try different paths. Or do all the multiplication problems first, and then choose your path.

Now cut out the puzzle piece. Decide where it goes in the puzzle frame on page 64. Glue or tape it in place.

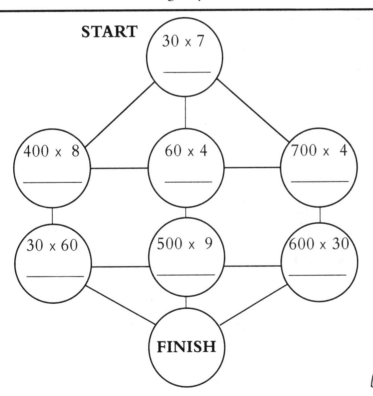

START

30 x 7
_____

400 x 8
_____

60 x 4
_____

700 x 4
_____

30 x 60
_____

500 x 9
_____

600 x 30
_____

FINISH

Check Yourself: When Bloog gets to the "Finish," he should have 27,710 asteroids. If he doesn't have that many, go back and try another route!

NAME _____

Homework Helper

Wilbur just finished doing his division homework. Can you help him decide if he has the right answers? Use multiplication to check each of Wilbur's answers. Give him 10 points for each correct answer. When you are done, write Wilbur's score here: _____

Multiplication is the opposite of division. So, to check division answers, work backward. Multiply the answer, or *quotient*, by the second number in the problem, the *divisor*. If your result is the number you started with, you know the division was done correctly.

A. $413 \div 7 = 59$

B. $288 \div 9 = 31$

C. $3,160 \div 5 = 632$

D. $816 \div 12 = 68$

E. $1428 \div 42 = 34$

F. $1,482 \div 26 = 55$

G. $2380 \div 35 = 68$

H. $3248 \div 4 = 812$

I. $2615 \div 5 = 523$

J. $2470 \div 38 = 64$

Work Space

Check Yourself: If you graded the homework correctly, Wilbur's total score should be a 70.

12

NAME_____

Racecar Remainders

**Start your engines! Then ask a friend or family member
to play this division game with you.**

Here's how:

1. Each player puts a small marker at "Start."
2. Spin to see who goes first. To use the spinner, spin a paper clip
   around the tip of a pencil, as shown in the picture on page 7.
3. Each player spins again, and moves that number of spaces.
4. For each turn after that, divide the number on your square by
   the number you spin. What is the remainder? Move ahead that
   many spaces. For example, say you are on the space marked
   "23" and you spin a 6. Since 23 ÷ 6 = 3 remainder 5, you
   move ahead 5 spaces.
5. If there is no remainder, stay put until your next turn.
6. The first person to zoom past the finish line wins!

> Here's a tip to help
> with division:
> Remember your
> times tables!
> For example,
> 9 x 3 = 27.
> So, you know that
> 28 ÷ 9 is 3 with a
> remainder of 1.

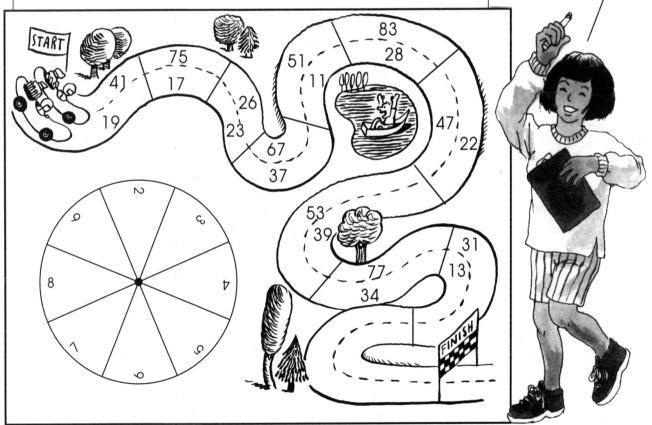

NAME _____

Tasty States

How would you like to live in Pie Town? Or maybe Spuds? Believe it or not, all the food names on this page are real places in the USA! Do the division below. Then find your answer in the State Box. Next to the correct answer is the name of the state where you can find that town. Write the correct state in each blank. One is done for you.

A. Pie Town is located in $(1,800 \div 3)$ ___600___ _New Mexico_

B. Spuds is in $(2,800 \div 40)$ _____

C. Beanville is in $(49,000 \div 70)$ _____

D. Noodle is in $(5,600 \div 100)$ _____

E. Jelly is in $(30,000 \div 500)$ _____

F. Oats is in $(64,000 \div 800)$ _____

G. Eggville is in $(56,000 \div 70)$ _____

State Box

Answer	State
70	Florida
60	California
600	New Mexico
56	Texas
700	Vermont
80	South Carolina
800	Mississippi

NAME_____

The Lunch Bunch

Linda, Max, Karen, and Willie are at a restaurant for lunch. How much will each of their meals cost? Add and subtract money amounts to find out!

Menu

Cheeseburger
$3.25

Tuna Sandwich
$2.85

French Fries
$1.25

Onion Rings
$1.79

Milk Shake
$1.62

Orange Juice
$1.50

1. If Max orders a cheeseburger and a milk shake, how much will his lunch cost?
   _____

2. Karen ordered a tuna sandwich and orange juice. How much was her lunch? _____

3. Linda's lunch order totaled $5.34, but the waiter forgot to bring her fries. If that charge is subtracted from the bill, how much will she pay? _____

4. Willie's order came to a total of $6.54, but he discovered that he only had $5.25. Karen offered to lend him the rest of the money he needed. How much will she have to lend him?_____

When you add or subtract money, don't forget to line up the decimal points in the problem.

It's time to cut out the puzzle piece. Glue or tape it in place on page 64.

Around the House: Next time you go to a restaurant, write down the prices of the food your family orders. Add them up to see what the bill will be before taxes are added on.

NAME _____

Time Troubles

Private detective Ima Snooper, at your service. Actually, today I'm at the service of Al Wayslate. His problem? He's never on time. So Al hired me to keep a record of what he does all day. Read the clocks in my notes to find out when Al did what. Write the correct time in the blank next to each clock. One is done for you.

> Remember a clock's little hand points to the hours. The big hand points to the minutes. Each little mark on the clock equals one minute.

On Friday, Al's parrot, Spot, started squawking at ⊙ __6:20__ in the morning. Al woke up and gave Spot some dog biscuits. Then he scattered birdseed on the floor for his puppy, Feathers. (I guess time isn't the only thing Al's confused about!) When he was finished, it was ⊙ _____. I followed Al to the bakery. First he looked at the donuts. Then he looked at the Danish. Then he looked at the coffee cake. Then he looked at the donuts again. By the time he decided to buy a muffin, it was ⊙ _____.

Al couldn't remember where he parked his car, so he decided to walk to work. By ⊙ _____, we were halfway there. Now, Al was hungry again! We stopped for lunch at Rocco's Tacos, and started walking again at ⊙ _____. Finally, we arrived at Al's office at ⊙ _____. It was so late, everyone else had already gone home for the day!

Around the House: Make a schedule of your day. Carry a pad of paper around with you. Write down the time for everything you do. Are you surprised how you spend your time?

NAME

Lloyd's Llamas

Welcome to Lloyd's Llama Farm! Today Lloyd is planning a birthday party for his favorite llama, Laura. As part of the decorations, Lloyd wants to string party lights around each llama pen. Help Lloyd find out how many feet of lights he should buy by writing the correct perimeter in the blank under each llama pen. One is done for you. Good luck!

Perimeter measures the distance around the outside of a shape. So, to find the perimeter of a shape, add the lengths of all the sides.

Pen A

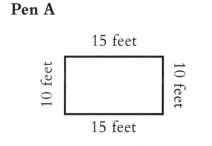

What is the perimeter of Pen A? __*50 feet*__

Pen B

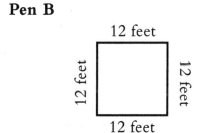

What is the perimeter of Pen B? _____

Pen C

What is the perimeter of Pen C? _____

Pen D

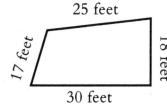

What is the perimeter of Pen D? _____

Check Yourself: To find out how many feet of lights Lloyd needs, add up the perimeters of Pens A, B, C, and D. The answer should be 252 feet.

NAME _____

Piece of Cake

The *area* of a shape is the amount of surface the shape covers. Area is measured in square units, like square inches or square feet. To find the area of a square or a rectangle, multiply the length times the width.

Today Lloyd baked 6 cakes for Laura Llama's birthday party. To make sure he will have enough cake for all the guests, he wants to find out the area of each cake. That will tell him how many square inches of cake there are. Write the correct area in the blank below each cake.

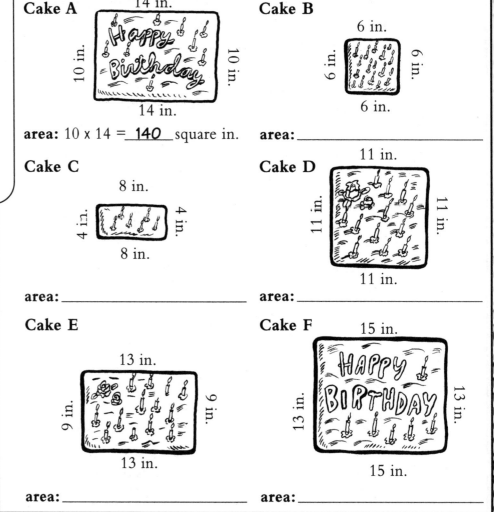

Cake A
14 in.
10 in.
10 in.
14 in.

area: 10 x 14 = __140__ square in.

Cake B
6 in.
6 in.
6 in.
6 in.

area: _____

Cake C
8 in.
4 in.
4 in.
8 in.

area: _____

Cake D
11 in.
11 in.
11 in.
11 in.

area: _____

Cake E
13 in.
9 in.
9 in.
13 in.

area: _____

Cake F
15 in.
13 in.
13 in.
15 in.

area: _____

Check Yourself: Add up the areas of Cakes A, B, C, D, E, and F. The total should be 641 square inches. Now that's a lot of cake!

NAME_____

Confetti Count

Lloyd ordered lots of boxes of confetti for Laura Llama's party. He stacked the boxes in cube shapes, with the same number of boxes stacked in rows across, up, and back. How many boxes does he have in all? To find out, help Lloyd calculate the volume of each stack. Write the correct volume in the blank under each stack of boxes.

> *Volume* is the amount of space inside a 3-dimensional shape. To find the volume of a cube, multiply length x width x height. Volume is measured in cubic units.

> Cut out the puzzle piece. Glue or tape it in place on page 64.

Stack A

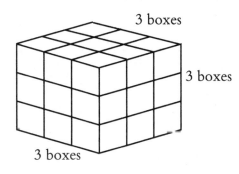

3 boxes

3 boxes

3 boxes

volume: 3 x 3 x 3 = __27__ cubic units

Stack B

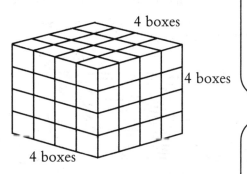

4 boxes

4 boxes

4 boxes

volume:_____

Stack C

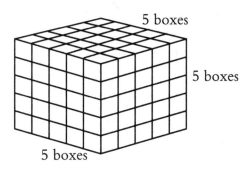

5 boxes

5 boxes

5 boxes

volume:_____

Stack D

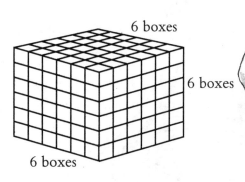

6 boxes

6 boxes

6 boxes

volume:_____

Check Yourself: Add up the volumes of Stacks A, B, C, and D. The total should be 432 cubic boxes.

NAME _____

Ship Shapes

Sharon and Shawn were carrying shapes in their ship.
When a big wave washed over the deck, the shapes got
knocked out of place! Sharon and Shawn drew dotted
lines around each shape before the wave hit. Look at the
position of each shape now. Then, use the dotted lines to
see where the shape was before. Depending on how it
moved, write "flip," "turn," "glide," or "dilation" in the
blank under each shape. One is done for you.

A *flip* flips a shape
over from one side
to another.
A *turn* spins the shape
around a point.

A *glide* slides a shape.
The size and shape
don't change.
In a *dilation*, the
shape shrinks or
stretches equally in all
directions. It looks the
same; it's just bigger
or smaller.

20

NAME_____

Gone Fishin'

Can you help Sharon and Shawn pick the best bait to catch each fish? If a fish's mouth makes a **right angle**, it likes worms best. If a fish's mouth makes any other kind of angle, it prefers minnows. Write the correct bait food in the blank under each fish. One is done for you.

Remember that an *angle* is formed when two lines, or rays, meet, like this:

In a *right angle*, the rays meet to form a corner like a square. You can test to see if an angle is a right angle by placing the corner of a sheet of paper on it. If the paper fits, it is a right angle.

Fish A
Type of bait: __*worms*__

Fish B
Type of bait: _____

Fish C
Type of bait: _____

Fish D
Type of bait: _____

Fish E
Type of bait: _____

Fish F
Type of bait: _____

Fish G
Type of bait: _____

Fish H
Type of bait: _____

NAME _____

Patty's Pizzas

At Patty's Pizza shop, fractions are always on the menu! Patty cuts up her pizzas in many different ways, but they're always cut into fractions! Under each pizza below, write the fraction that tells how much of the pizza is left on the pizza pan. One is done for you.

> A *fraction* is a part of a whole. The bottom number, or *denominator,* tells you how many pieces are in the whole. The top number, or *numerator,* tells you what portion of the whole you're talking about.

> If you cut a pizza into 4 equal pieces, and you take one of those pieces, you would have 3 pieces left. Those 3 out of 4 pieces would be called $\frac{3}{4}$ of the pizza.

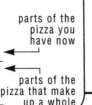

parts of the pizza you have now

$\frac{3}{4}$ ← parts of the pizza that make up a whole

1. What fraction of this pizza is left? $\frac{3}{6}$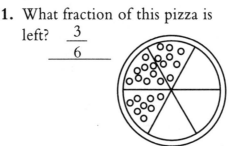

2. What fraction of this pizza is left? _____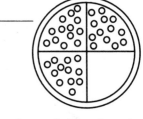

3. What fraction of this pizza is left? _____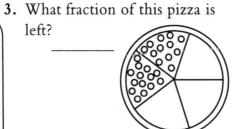

4. What fraction of this pizza is left? _____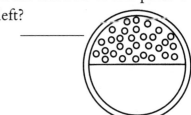

5. What fraction of this pizza is left? _____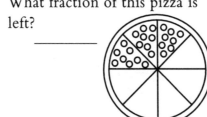

6. What fraction of this pizza is left? _____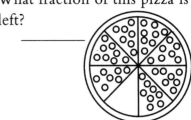

Around the House: Next time you eat a sandwich, cut it into quarters. Can you also cut it into eighths? What other foods do you know that can be divided into fractions?

NAME_____

Fraction Bingo

Ask a friend or family member to play Fraction Bingo with you. Here's how:

1. Each player uses a bingo card below. Take turns spinning. (To use the spinner, spin a paper clip around a pencil point.)
2. Find a fraction on your card that is equivalent to the fraction on the spinner. Mark an "X" over it. There is more than one equivalent fraction on the cards for each fraction on the spinner. But you can only "X" one box on each turn.
3. The first player to get 4 in a row across, down, or diagonally wins!

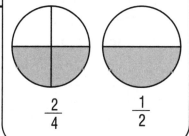

Two fractions are *equivalent,* or equal, if they stand for the same part of a whole. Can you see how $\frac{2}{4}$ and $\frac{1}{2}$ stand for the same part of the whole?

$\frac{2}{4}$ $\frac{1}{2}$

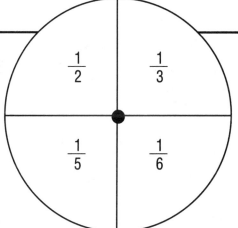

Bingo Card A

$\frac{2}{4}$	$\frac{5}{10}$	$\frac{2}{10}$	$\frac{6}{12}$
$\frac{3}{15}$	$\frac{2}{6}$	$\frac{3}{9}$	$\frac{2}{12}$
$\frac{4}{20}$	$\frac{3}{6}$	$\frac{4}{8}$	$\frac{4}{24}$
$\frac{2}{6}$	$\frac{2}{12}$	$\frac{3}{15}$	$\frac{4}{12}$

Bingo Card B

$\frac{3}{15}$	$\frac{3}{9}$	$\frac{5}{10}$	$\frac{4}{8}$
$\frac{2}{6}$	$\frac{6}{12}$	$\frac{2}{12}$	$\frac{4}{20}$
$\frac{3}{15}$	$\frac{4}{12}$	$\frac{2}{4}$	$\frac{2}{6}$
$\frac{4}{24}$	$\frac{2}{10}$	$\frac{2}{12}$	$\frac{3}{6}$

NAME _____

Watch the Birdies

Oops! Two baby birds, Bernice and Bertram, have fallen out of their nests. Can you help them get back in? Start at the bottom of the tree. When you get to a fork in the branches, take the branch with the greater fraction. Keep going until you reach the top. That will take you to Bernice's nest. To get to Bertram's nest, climb the tree again. This time, turn on each branch that has the smaller fraction.

Before you compare fractions, make sure the denominators are the same. The fraction with the higher numerator is greater. If the denominators aren't equal, try rewriting the fractions to make the denominators the same.

Cut out the puzzle piece. Put it in place on page 64.

Check Yourself: If you reached Bernice and Bertram's nests, you took the right paths. If not, go back and check your comparisons.

NAME_____

Fraction Action!

Places, everyone! The famous director Dim Jarmoose is filming his latest movie, "Last Fraction Hero." Before Dim finishes the movie, he needs your help to solve some fraction word problems. Write the answers on the lines. The first one is done for you.

1. Dim went to check on his 9 movie cameras. "Arrgh!" he yelled, upon discovering that 7 of them were broken.

   a. What fraction of the cameras was broken? ___ $\frac{7}{9}$ ___

   b. What fraction of the cameras was still working?_____

2. Dim noticed the light was too dim! Out of the 7 light bulbs he was using, 6 were burned out.

   a. What fraction of the bulbs was burned out?_____

   b. What fraction of the bulbs was working?_____

3. Dim sent the movie's animal trainer to buy more bulbs. While she was out, 12 of her 15 bunnies slipped through a hole in their cage!

   a. What fraction of the bunnies escaped?_____

   b. What fraction was left in the cage? _____

4. At lunchtime, Dim ordered a 5-foot submarine sandwich. He divided it into 10 equal parts. Dim ate 1 of the parts himself. The animal trainer ate 2. The star actress ate 3 parts. And the freed bunnies stole 4 parts for themselves!

   a. What fraction of the sandwich did Dim eat? _____

   b. What fraction of the sandwich did the animal trainer eat?_____

   c. What fraction of the sandwich did the actress eat?_____

   d. What fraction of the sandwich did the bunnies eat?_____

   e. Was any of the sandwich left over? _____

To help you solve each problem, try drawing a circle or a box around the numbers you need.

NAME _____

Grandparents Match

A *decimal* is a number with a small dot called a decimal point. To the right of the dot is one or more additional numbers.

Like a fraction, the part of a decimal to the right of the decimal point is a part of a whole. The first place to the right of the decimal point is called the tenths place. So, 0.1 is the same as $\frac{1}{10}$ and 1.6 is the same as $1\frac{6}{10}$

What do you call your grandparents? Grandma and Grandpa? Granny and Gramps? All around the world, kids have special names for their grandparents. Next to each country below is a decimal. Draw a line to match the decimal to its equivalent fraction. There you'll see a name that kids call their grandmother and grandfather in that country. One is done for you.

A.	Germany	2.3	$\frac{2}{10}$	Abuelita and Abuelito
B.	Japan	0.4	$1\frac{8}{10}$	Popo and Gong-gong
C.	Uganda	0.7	$\frac{7}{10}$	Jaja and Jaja
D.	Israel	0.9	$\frac{4}{10}$	Oba-chan and Oji-chan
E.	Mexico	0.2	$2\frac{3}{10}$	Oma and Opa
F.	Italy	3.4	$4\frac{3}{10}$	Ya-ya and Pa-pu
G.	India	7.1	$7\frac{1}{10}$	Nana-ji and Nani-ji
H.	Greece	4.3	$\frac{9}{10}$	Saba and Safta
I.	China	1.8	$3\frac{4}{10}$	Nonna and Nonno

26

NAME_____

Oh, Baby!

A baby horse is called a foal. A baby dog is a puppy. But what about a baby kangaroo? Next to each baby animal name below is a decimal. Circle the number that answers the question. That number will be next to the name of the grown-up animal. One is done for you.

Don't forget your decimal place value!

A. squeaker What number is in the tenths place of 25.86?

   2 mouse   **5** pig   (**8** pigeon)

B. kit What number is in the tenths place of 47.35?

   3 rabbit   **4** kangaroo   **7** lion

C. lamb What number is in the tenths place of 5.29?

   9 hippo   **5** opossum   **2** sheep

D. cheeper What number is in the tenths place of 302.68?

   8 owl   **6** quail   **3** parakeet

E. whelp What number is in the hundredths place of 8.97?

   8 whale   **9** gerbil   **7** tiger

F. elver What number is in the hundredths place of 52.04?

   4 eel   **0** moose   **5** elephant

G. joey What number is in the hundredths place of 731.65?

   7 deer   **5** kangaroo   **6** weasel

H. blinker What number is in the hundredths place of 452.09?

   9 mackerel   **4** zebra   **0** toucan

Check Yourself: Look at the numbers you circled. There should be one of each of these numbers: 2, 3, 4, 5, 6, 7, 8, 9. (The numbers aren't in order, though.)

Here's an example to keep in mind:

406.32

tenths
hundredths

NAME _____

Steffi's Graph

Steffi loves to play tennis. She also loves to draw graphs! Check out these graphs she created about her favorite game! Then take aim at the questions below.

> To read a picture graph, count the number of pictures. Look at the key to see how many items each picture stands for.

> To read a bar or line graph, look at the height of each bar or dot on the graph.

Steffi's Tennis Balls

Key

One 🎾 = 5 tennis balls

1. Steffi made this graph to show how many tennis balls she has in various colors. How many gray balls does Steffi have? _____
2. According to this graph, how many tennis balls does Steffi have in all? _____

Steffi's Tennis Practices

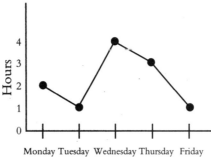

Steffi's Scores

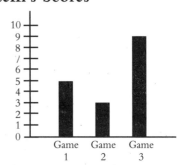

3. How many hours did Steffi practice on Monday?
   a. 4 hours   b. 2 hours
   c. 1 hour
4. On which day did Steffi practice the most?
   a. Friday   b. Tuesday
   c. Wednesday

5. How many points did Steffi score in Game 1?
   a. 5 points   b. 8 points
   c. 3 points
6. In what game was Steffi's score the lowest?
   a. Game 3   b. Game 1
   c. Game 2

Around the House: What's your favorite sport? Next time you play, make a graph about your scores or some other part of the game. What kind of graph will you choose?

NAME _____

Average Joe

Joe lives in an average town. He has average friends and an average dog. One thing about Joe is unusual, though. He always figures out the average of everything! Help Joe find averages for some of the things he saw yesterday. The first one has been done for you.

To find an average, start by adding up all the numbers in the set. Then, divide by how many numbers there are. Example: Find the average of 5, 12, and 4.
5 + 12 + 4 = 21
21 ÷ 3 = 7

1. This morning, Joe ate 2 pancakes. His mom ate 5 pancakes, his dad ate 6, and his sister ate 3. What was the average number of pancakes eaten? _____ *4 pancakes* _____

2. Joe counted the number of kids sitting in each of the first 7 rows on the school bus: 3, 1, 1, 2, 1, 3, and 3. What was the average number of kids in each row? _____

3. In math class, Joe noticed these 3 stacks of erasers:

What was the average number of erasers per stack? _____

4. On a field trip to the Botanical Gardens, he saw 5 beautiful flower beds. One bed had 12 roses, another had 10 tulips, a third had 19 mums, a fourth had 6 daisies, and the last bed had 3 pansies. What was the average number of flowers per bed? _____

Cut out the puzzle piece and find its place in the frame on page 64.

5. After school, Joe took his puppy Bowser to the park. Joe counted 5 poodles, 16 terriers, 2 Chihuahuas, 4 bulldogs, and 8 golden retrievers. What was the average number of dogs per breed that Joe counted? _____

Around the House: Ask family members to count various items on their dinner plates. Find the average number of each item.

NAME _____

Estimation Celebration!

Anita and Gilbert are throwing a party. They need to get an idea of about how much party stuff they've collected. Use estimation to help them find out! First, write and solve each problem using estimated numbers. Then find the estimated answer. One has been done for you.

One way to estimate is to round the numbers to the nearest tens before you add or subtract.

1. Anita bought 18 bags of potato chips. Gilbert bought 11 more bags. About how many bags do they have in all?
   Problem using estimation: _____ 20 + 10 _____
   Answer: _____ About 30 bags. _____

2. Gilbert collected 23 music tapes to play at the party. Anita gathered 18 more. About how many do they have in all?
   Problem using estimation: _____
   Answer: _____

3. Anita blew up 66 balloons. Gilbert blew up 53. About how many balloons do they have in all?
   Problem using estimation: _____
   Answer: _____

4. Gilbert bought 92 cans of soda. He and Anita got thirsty so they drank 9 cans. About how many cans are left?
   Problem using estimation: _____
   Answer: _____

5. Anita filled 83 bags with confetti for guests to throw. Her cat ripped open 24 of the bags! About how many are left?
   Problem using estimation: _____
   Answer: _____

Check Yourself: Look for each one of your answers in the following list: 40, 60, 80, 100, and 120. If your answer is not there, try the problem again!

NAME_____

Draw, Partner!

How can you solve a word problem with fractions? One way is to draw a picture. For each problem, draw a picture to help Cowgirl Carla solve a wild west question. Then answer the question.

1. Carla has a lot of cowboy hats. She keeps $\frac{1}{2}$ of the hats in her closet. She puts $\frac{1}{2}$ of the remaining hats in the living room. The hats that are left are hanging on hooks in the barn. What fraction of the hats is in the barn?_____ Draw a picture to solve the problem.

2. Carla's ranch hands had painted $\frac{1}{5}$ of the barn green when they ran out of paint. They used purple paint for $\frac{1}{2}$ of the part that was left. They then used red paint to finish painting the barn. What fraction of the barn was painted red?_____ Draw a picture to solve the problem.

3. Last week, Carla rode her horse, Louise, to the county fair. They were $\frac{1}{4}$ of the way there when Louise decided to stop and eat some grass. Then, they had traveled $\frac{2}{3}$ of the remaining distance by the time Louise wanted to stop and enjoy the sunshine. What fraction of the total distance did they have left to travel?_____ Draw a picture to solve the problem.

Here's a problem we solved by drawing a picture: Carla saw that $\frac{1}{3}$ of the chickens were pecking at seeds. Of the birds that were left, $\frac{1}{2}$ were running around clucking. The rest of the chickens were napping in the henhouse. What fraction of the chickens were napping?

To solve the problem, we drew this picture:

$\frac{1}{3}$ pecking	
$\frac{1}{2}$ running	remaining
$\frac{1}{3}$ napping	$\frac{2}{3}$

NAME _____

Eddie's Money

As an after-school job, Eddie runs a shopping service for his neighbors. But sometimes he can't remember how much money he's spent! For each problem below, help Eddie figure out how much money he has spent.

1. Eddie went to the fruit store for Mr. Hernandez. He spent $1.41 on figs. He bought bananas, too, but they cost three times as much as the figs. How much were the bananas?

   _____ 3 x $1.41 = $4.23 _____

2. Later, Eddie stopped at the hardware store for Mrs. Fong. He bought a hammer that cost $5.75. If he gave the clerk a ten-dollar bill, how much change did he receive?

   _____

3. When he went to the grocery store for Mr. Williams, Eddie bought 3 boxes of breakfast cereal at $3.56 a box. He also bought 2 cans of soup for $.45 a can. How much did Eddie spend at the grocery store?

   _____

4. On the way home, Eddie stopped by the candy store to buy himself a few treats. He wanted to buy a chocolate bar for $.82, a stick of licorice for $.24, and a piece of bubble gum for $.18. He had $1.10. Was this enough money to buy these items?_____

   How much more money did he need?_____

Cut out the piece and decide where it fits on page 64.

Problem
Solving

Calculate area
and volume
using tiles
and cubes

NAME

Square Off

What's the area of the shapes below? One way to find
out is to see how many square centimeter tiles will fit
inside them. Carefully cut out the square centimeter tiles
at the right along the dotted lines. Then, fill up each
shape below with the tiles to find each shape's area in
square centimeters.

**CENTIMETER
TILES**

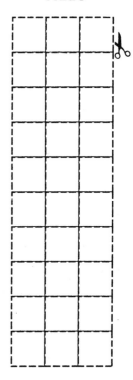

Shape A

Area:_____ square centimeters

Shape B

Area:_____ square centimeters

Shape C

Shape D

Area:_____ square centimeters   Area:_____ square centimeters

Check Yourself: To check your answers for shapes A, B,
and C, use the tiles to measure how tall and wide each shape is
in centimeters. Multiply the two numbers. The answer should
match your answer for the area of the shape.

NAME _____

Join the Millions Club!

Keisha and her friends started a Millions Club. Everyone who joins must pick a number over one million to serve as a secret number. To find Keisha's secret number, follow the directions below. We did the first one for you.

Circle the number in the . . .

A. Millions place of Ted's number: 4②,934,810

B. Ten millions place of Cindy's number: 683,739,251

C. Hundred millions place of Shu's number: 527,149,003

D. Ten millions place of Maria's number: 301,564,299

E. Millions place of Jason's number: 34,366,502

F. Hundred millions place of Robin's number: 700,628,943

G. Hundred millions place of Louie's number: 161,030,825

H. Millions place of Michelle's number: 389,402,633

I. Ten millions place of Eric's number: 41,903,014

Write each number you circled on the correct blank:

$$\overline{A} \ \ \overline{B} \ \ \overline{C}\, ' \ \ \overline{D} \ \ \overline{E} \ \ \overline{F}\, ' \ \ \overline{G} \ \ \overline{H} \ \ \overline{I}$$

Check Yourself: Did you write this number: two hundred eighty-five million, forty seven thousand, one hundred ninety-four?

Around the House: Ask family members what numbers they would choose for their secret numbers in the Millions Club. Don't forget your number. Write each number, and then order them from least to greatest.

Numeration

Compare and order
up to hundreds of
thousands

NAME_____

Step To It!

On a school trip to a shoe factory, Jeff got separated
from his class. Help him find his way back to the school
bus! Jeff can step to the next shoe in any direction from
where he's standing, but for each step, he must choose
the shoe with the greater number on it. As you go, draw
a line to trace Jeff's path.

> To compare large
> numbers, start with
> the highest place
> value. If they are
> equal, then look at the
> next place value.
>
> **Examples:**
> 345,800
> is greater than
> 34,580
>
> 672,324
> is greater than
> 668,324

JEFF

21,664

14,721

12,466

140,721

480,731

321,703

307,973

498,612

496,812

633,843

633,734

520,172

840,599

BUS

SCHOOL BUS

Check Yourself: It should take Jeff 6 steps to get back to
the bus. If not, go back and try again!

NAME _____

Hundred Hunt

Where did that darn kitty get to? Rachel is looking for her cat, Alberta. The kitty will usually come if Rachel counts by 100s. Today, she's already counted to 500, and Alberta's still hiding! Use this maze to help Rachel continue counting. As you count, move to the square with the correct number in it. You can move up, down, to the side, or diagonally. The maze is started for you.

Way to go! Now you can cut out the puzzle piece. Figure out where it goes in the puzzle frame on page 64. Then glue or tape it in place.

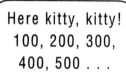

Here kitty, kitty! 100, 200, 300, 400, 500 . . .

START

600	900	1,100	700	300	1,100
500	700	600	1,100	1,200	400
800	1,200	1,000	900	1,000	1,300
700	900	1,600	1,500	1,400	500
100	800	1,700	1,300	1,900	1,600
900	1,000	200	1,800	1,700	2,000

END

NAME_____

Farm Funnies

To find the answer to this riddle, round the number
below each line to the nearest thousands place. Look
for the rounded number in the Rounding Box. Next
to it, you'll find a letter of the alphabet. Write it on
the line. (Hint: Some letters are used more then once.
Some won't be used at all.)

To round to
the nearest
thousands place,
round up if the
hundreds place
is 5 or greater.
If it is less than
5, round down.

Riddle: Where does a cow go to eat lunch?
Riddle Answer: A cow eats lunch in the . . .

___ ___ ___ ___ ___ ___ ___ ___ ___ ___
4,120 7,998 2,007 5,500 1,070 9,237 965 6,793 4,508 8,445

Rounding Box								
1,100	Q		1,000	E		6,000	F
4,000	C		70,000	P		900	U
8,400	J		3,000	M		2,000	L
7,000	R		9,000	T		5,000	I
8,000	A		4,500	W			

NAME _____

Palindrome Pals

Palindromes read the same way forward and backward. Know anyone named "Anna?" That's one example! In this puzzle, all the answers are number palindromes! For example, 5,665 is a number palindrome. Do the math for each problem. Then write your answer in the cross-number puzzle. We did one for you.

Across

A. 30,712
   + 11,202

E. 56,542
   + 21,945

G. 62,988
   + 35,301

I. 88,881
   − 62,819

Down

B. 5,211
   − 4,747

C. 12,538
   + 20,185

D. 26,388
   + 29,567

F. 12,009
   − 11,181

H. 64,553
   − 64,281

A. 4	1	9	1	B. 4	■	C.
■	■	■			■	
D.	■	E.	F.			
	■			■		
G.		H.				
	■		■	■	■	■
	■	I.				

Check Yourself: Does each number in your completed puzzle read the same way forwards and backwards?

Around the House: On a separate piece of paper, make up your own cross-number puzzle. Ask a family member to solve it!

NAME_____

What a Card!

All the cards below are mixed up. Do all of the math problems, then cut them out along the dotted line. Move them around until each card is telling the truth. For example, one card points up and says: "52 x 16." Since 52 x 16 = 832, that card must be pointing to the card with the number 832 on it. Find that card and put it in the right place. But before you start the puzzle, turn to the top of page 40 for an extra hint.

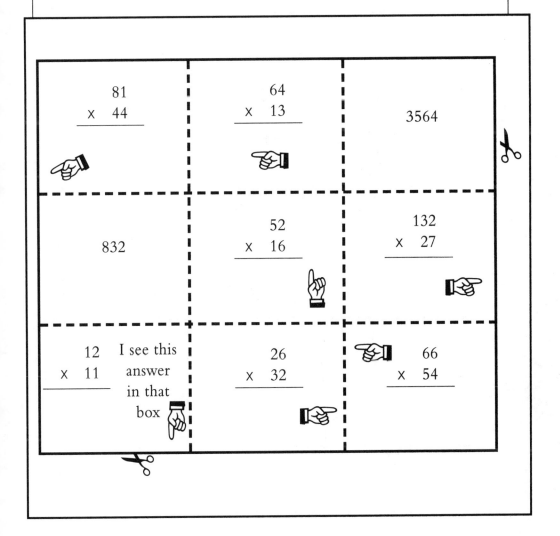

NAME _____

What a Card!

When you are done moving the cards around, they should form a square with 3 cards on each side. Tape the cards together in the new square.

Flip the whole puzzle over. Check to see if the math works on the other side. If it does, you did the puzzle correctly.
If not, cut the tape and try again!

It's puzzle time! Cut out the piece and put it on page 64.

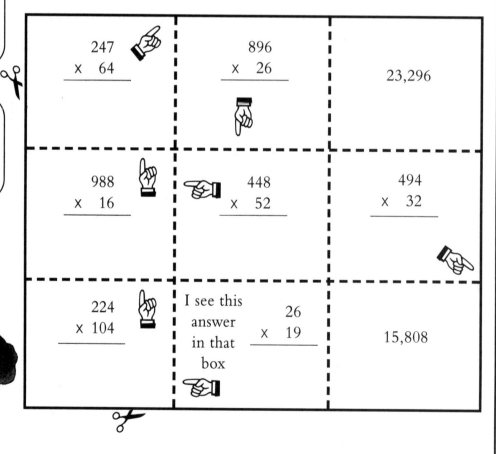

NAME_____

Fill 'er Up!

Fill in the empty squares below so that all the division problems are true. First, do each problem going across. Write your answer in the empty square. Then do each problem going down. When you are done, use your answers to do the division problems going across the bottom row and down the right-hand column. One is done for you.

Here's a hint: Do your division on a separate piece of paper.

6,912	÷	72	=	**96**
÷	■	÷	■	÷
96	÷	12	=	
=	■	=	■	=
	÷		=	

7,168	÷	64	=	
÷	■	÷	■	÷
112	÷	16	=	
=	■	=	■	=
	÷		=	

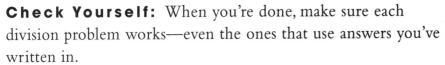

Also, don't forget to set up each problem like this:

72)‾6,912

Check Yourself: When you're done, make sure each division problem works—even the ones that use answers you've written in.

NAME _____

Round Off, One, Two!

Terence Tuna and Christine Cod just joined the Fish Marines! Their first assignment is to make sure the Mess Hall has enough food for each meal. Here's how:

1. Round the number of cans of fish food to the nearest hundred.
2. Round the number of Fish Marines to the nearest ten.
3. Use your rounded numbers to do the division. Then you'll know about how many cans of food each fish will get to eat! Terence and Christine did the first one for you.

> Remember:
> If you don't need an exact answer, you can make the problem easier by rounding.

> To divide 379 by 48, first round 379 to 400. Then round 48 to 50. Use the rounded numbers to divide: $400 \div 50 = 8$. So $379 \div 48$ is about 8.

1. For breakfast on Monday, the chef set aside 821 cans of fish food. There will be 78 Marines at the meal.
   Original problem: $821 \div 78$
   Using rounded numbers:
   $$800 \div 80 = 10$$
   About how many cans of food will each fish get to eat? _____ 10

2. For Monday's lunch, there are 697 food cans. There will be 52 Marines at the meal.
   Original problem: $697 \div 52$
   Using rounded numbers:
   _____
   About how many cans of food will each fish get?_____
   _____

3. On Tuesday, there are 917 cans of food for dinner. There will be 88 Marines at the meal.
   Original problem: _____
   Using rounded numbers:
   _____
   About how many cans will each fish get? _____

4. For lunch on Thursday, there are 1,389 cans of food. There will be 72 Marines at the meal.
   Original problem:
   Using rounded numbers:
   _____
   How many cans will each fish get?_____

42

NAME

School Daze

Ogden Octopus wants your help in dividing up the pencils for his Fish School! He's already done the division. He wants you to use multiplication to check his work, adjusting his answers if necessary. One is done for you.

1. Class A has 289 pencils and 26 fishy students. About how many pencils are there for each student?

   a. Original problem:
      289 ÷ 26

   b. Using rounded numbers:
      300 ÷ 30 = 10

   c. Check the answer:

      10 x 26 = 260

      289 – 260 = 29

   d. Adjust your answer if necessary:

      29 is greater than 26,

      so the adjusted answer

      is: 289 ÷ 26 = about 11

2. Class B has 875 pencils and 45 students. About how many pencils are there for each student?

   a. Original problem:
      875 ÷ 45

   b. Using rounded numbers:
      900 ÷ 50 = 18

   c. Check the answer:

      _____

      _____

   d. Adjust your answer if necessary:

      _____

3. Class C has 214 pencils and 21 students. About how many pencils are there for each student?

   a. Original problem:
      214 ÷ 21

   b. Using rounded numbers:
      200 ÷ 20 = 10

   c. Check your answer:

      _____

      _____

   d. Adjust your answer if necessary:

      _____

To find 335 ÷ 46, you round to make the problem easier: 300 ÷ 50 = 6. This means your first estimate will be 6. Now check this estimate by multiplying 6 x 46. Did you get 276?

Is 276 as close as you can get to 335? To find out, subtract: 335 – 276. You'll get 59, and 59 is greater than 46. That means 46 could have gone into 335 one more time. So instead of 6, adjust the answer: 335 ÷ 46 is about 7.

Grade 4

43

NAME _____

Wacky Cash

Long ago, people used all kinds of things for money. To find out where each odd kind of money was used, multiply the money amount for each problem. Find your answer in the Answer Box. Write it in the blank. One is done for you.

Multiply money just as you would multiply any other numbers. Then put a decimal point two places to the left in your answer.

A. $4.31
  x   3
  ‾‾‾‾‾‾
  $12.93

Bags of salt were money in ___Ancient Rome___ .

B. $2.00
  x   4
  ‾‾‾‾‾‾

Porpoise teeth were money in _____ .

C. $3.42
  x   2
  ‾‾‾‾‾‾

Fish hooks were money in _____ .

D. $6.89
  x   7
  ‾‾‾‾‾‾

Cocoa beans were money in _____ .

E. $9.35
  x   6
  ‾‾‾‾‾‾

Tea cakes were money in _____ .

F. $3.87
  x   10
  ‾‾‾‾‾‾

Playing cards were used as money in _____ .

Answer Box			
$56.10	Ancient China	$38.70	Canada
$ 6.84	Alaska	$12.93	Ancient Rome
$ 8.00	Fiji Islands	$48.23	16th century Mexico

NAME_____

"Al" Be Back

Detective Ima Snooper here. Poor Al Wayslate! He's
having problems with time, so he wants me to figure out
how much time he spent doing each activity in his day.
Use my notes to solve the problems below. Maybe then
Al will figure out what he's doing wrong.

Remember: there
are 60 minutes in
an hour. Also, be
careful when you
figure out a
problem that goes
from a.m. to p.m.

1. At 7:30 a.m., Al took his parrot Spot out
for a walk. They returned home at 9:00 a.m.
How long were they out walking?
_____ hours, _____ minutes.

2. At 9:15 a.m. Al decided to make breakfast.
He stuck his head into the refrigerator to see
what food was in there. Al kept looking until
11:30 a.m. when he finally decided to eat 2
bananas and some leftover macaroni. How
much time did Al spend looking through the
refrigerator?_____ hours, _____ minutes.

3. Al started eating at 11:30 a.m. By 1:39
p.m., he was finished. How much time did Al
spend eating?_____hours, _____ minutes.

Good work!
You're ready for
the big time!
But now it's
puzzle time.

4. At 1:45 p.m., Al began washing the dishes with a toothbrush!
The brush was so small that he didn't finish the job until 5:15 p.m. How
long did it take Al to wash the dishes? _____ hours, _____minutes.

5. Washing the dishes tired Al out, so he decided to take a nap. Al
fell asleep at 6:03 p.m. and woke up at 10:21 p.m. How long
did Al sleep?_____ hours, _____ minutes.

Around the House: The next time you go to school,
write down the time you leave your home. Then write down
the time you arrive at school. How long did the trip take?

Geometry

Study quadrilaterals, parallelograms, and rhombuses

NAME _____

Yummy Shapes

> A *quadrilateral* is any shape that has 4 sides. There are many kinds of quadrilaterals. A *parallelogram* is a special quadrilateral with 2 pairs of parallel sides. (Look on page 49 to see what *parallel* means.) A *rhombus* is a parallelogram with 4 equal sides.

"Give me a squeeze!" yells a waiter to the cook in a restaurant. He's using "diner slang" to order a glass of orange juice. You can find out what more diner slang means below. For each problem, circle the correct shape. The name of the real food is in the shape.

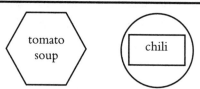

tomato soup   chili

1. In diner slang, a "bowl of red" is . . .
(**Hint:** The correct answer is in the *quadrilateral.*)

lettuce and tomato   salt and pepper

2. If a waitress asks for "Mike and Ike," she means . . .
(**Hint:** The correct answer is in the *parallelogram.*)

water   lemonade

3. "City juice" is a way of saying . . .
(**Hint:** The correct answer is in the *parallelogram.*)

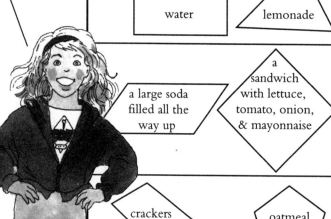

a large soda filled all the way up   a sandwich with lettuce, tomato, onion, & mayonnaise

4. An "all the way" is . . .
(**Hint:** The correct answer is in the *rhombus.*)

crackers   oatmeal cookies

5. "Dog biscuits" are . . .
(**Hint:** The correct answer is in the *quadrilateral.*)

an English muffin   a cup of tea

6. "British" means . . .
(**Hint:** The correct answer is in the *rhombus.*)

46

NAME_____

Polygon Giggles

Here's a joke about geometry: How did the shapes get to school? To find the answer to this riddle, fill in the chart below. Read the name of each polygon and the number of sides it has. Find the polygon on the page. Then write the letter inside the polygon on the correct line. Then, flip to page 48 and follow the directions.

Polygon	Number of Sides	Letter
Triangle	3	_____
Quadrilateral	4	_____
Pentagon	5	_____
Hexagon	6	_____
Heptagon	7	_____
Octagon	8	_____
Nonagon	9	_____
Decagon	10	_____
Dodecagon	12	_____

N
R
S
O
M

Did you know that a *polygon* is any closed shape made up of straight lines?

And polygons have different names depending on how many sides they have. Look at the list.

 O
 U
 A
 H
 B

NAME _____

More Polygon Giggles

Look at the chart on page 47. Write the correct letter on the line above the name of the polygon. When you're finished, the letters will spell out the answer to the riddle!

You got those all sorted out! Here is another puzzle piece to cut out and glue or tape in place. Any ideas what the picture is yet?

_____   _____   _____   _____
Hexagon   Triangle   Quadrilateral   Octagon

_____   _____   _____
Pentagon   Hexagon   Decagon

_____   _____   _____
Heptagon   Dodecegon   Nonagon

NAME

Kick It!

Shelley and David like to play soccer together. They take turns kicking soccer balls. The paths the balls travel form parallel or perpendicular lines. Look at the pictures below. Then answer the question or follow the directions below each picture.

1. Are the paths parallel or perpendicular?

_____

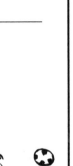

2. Are the paths parallel or perpendicular?

_____

Remember, *perpendicular* lines meet to form right angles.

perpendicular lines

3. Draw a line to show how Shelley could kick a ball that would travel perpendicular to David's kick.

4. Draw a line to show how David could kick a ball that would travel parallel to Shelley's kick.

Parallel lines, however, never meet.

parallel lines

Around the House: Look at a piece of lined notebook paper. Are the lines parallel or perpendicular? Can you find any other examples of parallel or perpendicular lines?

NAME _____

Similar Critters

When many of the same kind of animal are together, the group has a special name. We've listed some animal group names below. For problems 1 to 3, you can find the correct answer by looking at the word inside a congruent shape. For problems 4 to 6, you'll find the answers by looking for a similar shape. Draw a line from each special name to the correct animals. One is done for you.

Remember: *Congruent shapes* have exactly the same shape and size.

Similar figures have the same shape, but their sizes are different.

Find the congruent shape:

1. A paddling of . . .

2. A crash of . . .

3. A howl of . . .

hyenas

rhinoceroses

pandas

ducks

hounds

bulls

Find the similar shape:

4. A pounce of . . .

5. A float of . . .

6. A crackle of . . .

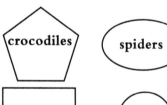

crocodiles

spiders

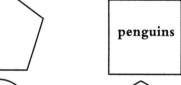

penguins

crickets

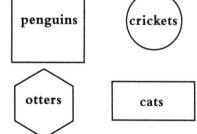

otters

cats

50

Grade 4

NAME_____

Ring Around the Circle

Welcome to the Roundville County Fair! At this fair, there are lots of things in the official shape of the county. Can you guess what that shape is? You're right— the circle. How many circles can you find? Put a check next to each circle you see. If the circle has a diameter or radius marked on it, write "diameter" or "radius" to label it. One is done for you.

You can find circles just about anywhere! A *circle* is a round shape like a plate.

A line that cuts a circle exactly in half is called a *diameter*. A line between the center of a circle and the outside of the circle is called a *radius*. Here's an example:

Around the House: How many radii would there be in a pizza for your family? Count them next time you have pizza.

NAME _____

Gulp Some Gorp

Time for a delicious snack. How about gorp—"good old raisins and peanuts." How much should you make? That depends on how many people you want to serve. The recipe below serves 4 people. To find out how much of each ingredient you'd need to serve more or less than 4, just add and subtract the fractions below. One is done for you.

Do you remember how to add fractions? If the denominators are the same, just add the numerators. Here's an example:

$$\frac{1}{5} + \frac{2}{5} = \frac{3}{5}$$

You're ready to cut out the puzzle piece. Glue or tape it in place in the frame on page 64.

Make the Recipe Bigger

Ingredient	Serves 4	Serves 6
Sunflower seeds	$\frac{2}{6}$ cup + $\frac{1}{6}$ cup =	$\frac{3}{6}$ cup
Raisins	$\frac{2}{4}$ cup + $\frac{1}{4}$ cup =	_____
Peanuts	$\frac{2}{3}$ cup + $\frac{1}{3}$ cup =	_____
Granola	1 cup ($\frac{2}{2}$) + $\frac{1}{2}$ cup =	_____
M&Ms	$\frac{2}{3}$ cup + $\frac{1}{3}$ cup =	_____

Make the Recipe Smaller

Ingredient	Serves 4	Serves 2
Sunflower seeds	$\frac{2}{6}$ cup − $\frac{1}{6}$ cup =	_____
Raisins	$\frac{2}{4}$ cup − $\frac{1}{4}$ cup =	_____
Peanuts	$\frac{2}{3}$ cup − $\frac{1}{3}$ cup =	_____
Granola	1 cup ($\frac{2}{2}$) − $\frac{1}{2}$ cup =	_____
M&Ms	$\frac{2}{3}$ cup − $\frac{1}{3}$ cup =	_____

Around the House: Ask a grownup to help you make your own gorp! Change the recipe if you like. What ingredients would you like to add? What would you leave out?

52

Grade 4

NAME_____

Pie Parts

Carmen loves pie. Every day, she visits her favorite pie shop, Pies "R" Us, where pies are sold by the slice. Carmen uses mixed fractions to count how much of each kind of pie the store has left. Help her tally up today's pies. The first one is done for you.

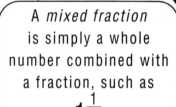

A *mixed fraction* is simply a whole number combined with a fraction, such as
$$1\frac{1}{2}$$
You would say that number: "One and one-half." It means you have one whole plus another $\frac{1}{2}$ of a whole.

1. How many apple pies are there?
   Count these pies. _____ $3\frac{3}{8}$ apple pies

2. How many cherry pies are there?
   Count these pies. _____

3. How many blueberry pies are there?
   Count these pies. _____

4. How many strawberry pies are there?
   Count these pies. _____

5. How many pumpkin pies are there?
   Count these pies. _____
   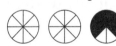

To compare mixed fractions, look at the whole number first. The mixed fraction with the larger whole number is greater. If the whole numbers are the same, then you compare the fractions.

Bonus: Write the pie names and amounts in order from least to greatest here: _____

_____

Around the House: What can you count using mixed fractions? Can you find $2\frac{1}{2}$ pairs of socks? Can you drink $1\frac{1}{3}$ cups of water?

NAME _____

Decimal Dance-a-thon

To compare decimals, start with the tenths place. If the number in the tenths place is 5 or more, round up. If not, round down. If the tenths place is the same for both numbers, then look at the hundredths place. Then round up or down.

Here's your puzzle piece. Put it in place on page 64.

The Decimal Dancers are about to put on a show! To decide who gets to dance first, each couple has picked a decimal number. The numbers are written out in words. Rewrite each decimal as a number. One has been started for you.

Seventy-three hundredths   Babs and Doug's decimal _.73_

four tenths   Rae and Ted's decimal _____

forty-seven hundredths   John and Paula's decimal _____

thirty-seven hundredths   Viola and Stan's decimal _____

seven tenths   Rob and Laura's decimal _____

Now write the decimals in order from least to greatest. Put the dancers' names next to their decimals to show the order in which the couples will dance.

1. Decimal: _____ Dancers: _____

2. Decimal: _____ Dancers: _____

3. Decimal: _____ Dancers: _____

4. Decimal: _____ Dancers: _____

5. Decimal: _____ Dancers: _____

NAME_____

Math Laugh

Math is no joke, but you'll need math to find the answer to this riddle! For each problem, add or subtract the decimals. Then find the decimal answer in the riddle answer below. Write the letter of the problem on that line. When you're finished, the answer to the riddle will be spelled out. The first problem has been done for you.

D. $\begin{array}{r} 1.32 \\ +\ .79 \\ \hline 2.11 \end{array}$

A. $\begin{array}{r} 4.73 \\ +2.19 \\ \hline \end{array}$

A. $\begin{array}{r} 0.41 \\ +0.32 \\ \hline \end{array}$

E. $\begin{array}{r} 5.32 \\ -0.2 \\ \hline \end{array}$

E. $\begin{array}{r} 0.82 \\ -0.11 \\ \hline \end{array}$

H. $\begin{array}{r} 4.05 \\ +1.25 \\ \hline \end{array}$

H. $\begin{array}{r} 3.45 \\ +0.26 \\ \hline \end{array}$

C. $\begin{array}{r} 4.2 \\ -1.01 \\ \hline \end{array}$

A. $\begin{array}{r} 7.91 \\ -0.68 \\ \hline \end{array}$

Remember, when you add or subtract decimals, you must line up the decimal points.

RIDDLE: If you tried to add all the numbers from one to one thousand, then multiply your answer by one million, and finally divide this answer by one billion, what would you get?

Answer:

$\overline{}\ \ \overline{}\ \ \overline{}\ \ \overline{}\ \ \overset{D}{\overline{}}\ \ \overline{}\ \ \overline{}\ \ \overline{}\ \ \overline{}$

7.23   5.30   5.12   0.73   2.11   6.92   3.19   3.71   0.71

NAME _____

Take a Number

Benny's Bread Shop is always busy. To keep track of the customers who are waiting to be served, Benny draws number lines. Help Benny draw number lines for some of today's customers. The first one has been done for you.

A number line starts at the left. Each mark to the right on the number line is one number greater.

1. When Benny opened the shop 6 people were waiting outside. They each came in and took a number, starting with "0." What number line did Benny draw?

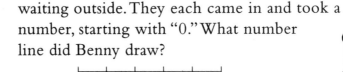

2. At 8:30 a.m., there were 4 people in line. The first person held the number 12. Draw a number line for this group of customers.

3. By noon, 6 people had lined up to buy rolls for their lunch sandwiches. The last person in line held the number 73. Draw a number line for this group of customers.

4. That afternoon, Benny ran out of numbers. He had to start a new batch, beginning with "0." What did his number line look like when the first 7 people with new numbers lined up?

5. Benny decided to put sweet buns on sale. The first person in line had the number 43. The last person had number 58. Draw a number line for this group of customers.

   How many people were in this line? _____
   Use your number line to count.

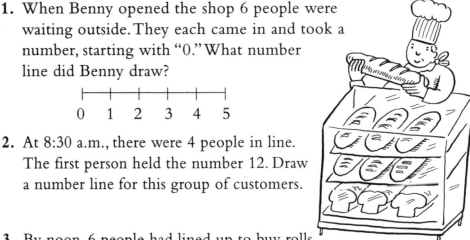

56

NAME _____

Lila's Lap

Splash! Lila spends most her time in the water. But, when she's not paddling back and forth, you'll find her by the side of the pool making line graphs. Use the chart below to help Lila make a line graph about her laps across the pool. She started the graph for you.

To plot points on this line graph, start with the first day, and find the number of laps Lila swam on that day. Mark the point. Then do the same thing for each of the other days.

Lila's Swimming Data

Day 1: 4 laps	Day 2: 3 laps	Day 3: 6 laps
Day 4: 5 laps	Day 5: 7 laps	Day 6: 4 laps

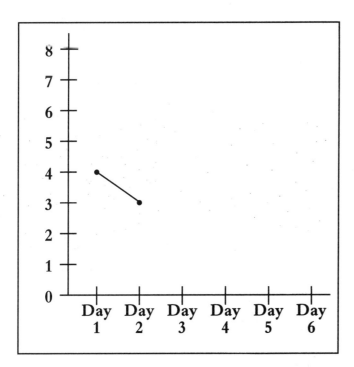

When you've marked all the points, draw a line to connect them.

Check Yourself: If you completed the graph correctly, the line should go down, up, down, up, down. If not, check your points again!

NAME_____

Fair's Fair

Everyone knows that games are more fun when they're fair. Are the games below fair? For each spinner, decide whether the probability of spinning stripes or polka dots is equal. If the probability is the same, circle "FAIR." If not, circle "UNFAIR." One has been done for you.

A *probability* is a number that tells you the chance that an event will happen.

For example, say there are 10 equal sections on a spinner. 3 of them have stripes and 7 of them have polka dots. The probability of spinning stripes is 3 out of 10, or $\frac{3}{10}$. The probability of spinning dots is $\frac{7}{10}$. Because $\frac{7}{10}$ is greater than $\frac{3}{10}$, the probability of spinning polka dots is greater.

Spinner A: FAIR or (UNFAIR?)

Spinner B: FAIR or UNFAIR?

Spinner C: FAIR or UNFAIR?

Spinner D: FAIR or UNFAIR?

Spinner E: FAIR or UNFAIR?

Spinner F: FAIR or UNFAIR?

Check Yourself: To check your answers, try spinning each spinner 20 times.
Spin a paper clip around a pencil like this:

Keep track of your results. Does each pattern come up about the same number of times?

58

NAME_____

Flipping Out!

Can you predict how many times a flipped penny will come up heads? Take your chances and find out!

1. **a.** If you flip a coin 10 times, how many times do you think it will come up heads?

   Theoretical trial: _____

   b. Get a penny. Flip it 10 times. How many times did it come up heads?

   Experimental trial: _____

2. **a.** If you flip the penny 20 times, how many times do you think it will come up heads?

   Theoretical trial: _____

   b. Try flipping the penny 20 times. How many times did heads come up this time?

   Experimental trial: _____

3. **a.** What if you flipped 2 pennies at once? If you flip them 20 times, how many times do you think they will both come up heads?

   Theoretical trial: _____

   b. Now, go ahead and flip two pennies at once, 20 times. How many times did they both come up heads at the same time?

   Experimental trial: _____

Here are some definitions to help you with this activity. A *trial* is when an event happens, like flipping a coin that comes up heads.

A *theoretical trial* is your prediction of how many times the penny will come up heads if you flip it several times. An *experimental trial* is when you test the theory by flipping the penny that many times.

**Problem
Solving**

Estimate length
in inches,
feet and
yards

NAME _____

Give Yourself a Hand!

What can you do if you need to measure something, but you don't have a ruler handy? You could use your hand as a measuring tool. Practice your "handy" measuring to answer the questions below. Then, find the estimated measurement in inches, feet, and yards.

Remember, there are 12 inches in one foot. And there are 3 feet in one yard!

Here's a puzzle piece. Cut it out and put it where it belongs on page 64.

1. Place your hand, from wrist to fingertip, along each object.

   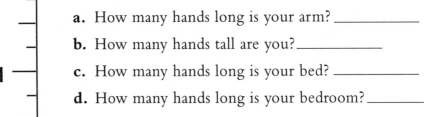

   a. How many hands long is your arm? _____

   b. How many hands tall are you? _____

   c. How many hands long is your bed? _____

   d. How many hands long is your bedroom? _____

2. Measure your hand in inches. Lay it along the ruler at the right. Rounded to the nearest inch, how long is your hand?

   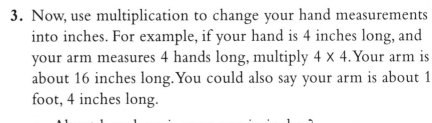

   _____

3. Now, use multiplication to change your hand measurements into inches. For example, if your hand is 4 inches long, and your arm measures 4 hands long, multiply 4 X 4. Your arm is about 16 inches long. You could also say your arm is about 1 foot, 4 inches long.

   a. About how long is your arm in inches? _____

   b. About how tall are you in feet and inches? _____

   c. About how long is your bed in feet and inches? _____

   d. About how long is your bedroom in yards, feet, and inches? _____

A Super Bowl

Ready to do some tasty estimation? First, ask a parent or another adult to help you gather the supplies. Then follow the directions below.

What you need:
- A small cup or glass
- A large bowl
- A napkin or paper towel
- A box of Cheerios or another cereal that comes in small pieces (the box should be bigger than the bowl)

What to do:

1. Fill your cup with cereal.

2. Dump the cup out onto the paper towel. Count the cereal pieces. How many pieces are there? _____

3. Fill your cup with cereal again. Dump it into the bowl.

4. Keep filling your cup and dumping it into the bowl until the bowl is full. How many times did you dump a cup of cereal into the bowl? _____

5. Multiply your answer from question 4 by your answer from question 2. That will tell you about how many cereal pieces are in the big bowl. Answer: _____

6. Do you think the answer you got in question 5 is an exact answer or an estimate?

_____

Explain your thinking. _____

_____

_____

_____

7. Put the cereal back in the box when you're all done.

NAME _____

Cow-abunga!

Convert these metric measurements to find the answer to a cow riddle. When you're finished, you'll be laughing all the way to the barn! For each problem, circle the letter next to the correct answer. Write that letter in the blank above the number of the problem. One has been done for you.

Here are some metric measurements to remember:

1 kilometer (km) = 1,000 meters (m)	
1 meter	= 100 centimeters (cm)
1 meter	= 1,000 millimeters (mm)
1 centimeter	= 10 millimeters

1. How many cm are in 5 m? **A** 50 **O** 500

2. How many mm are in 3 cm? **U** 30 **S** 300

3. How many km are there in 5,000 m? **L** 50 **M** 5

4. How many cm are in 800 mm? **S** 80 **A** 8

5. How many cm are in 7 m? **Q** 7,000 **E** 700

6. How many m are in 6,000 cm? **O** 60 **I** 6

7. How many cm are in 1 km? **M** 100,000 **B** 1,000

Riddle: Where do cows go to look at famous works of art?

Answer: To a...

__ __ O - __ __ __ __!
7 6 1   4 5 2 3

Remember, when you are changing from a big unit to a smaller unit, you must multiply. When changing from a small unit to a bigger unit, you have to divide.

NAME_____

Chatterbox Charlie

Charlie wants to tell you all about his trip to the circus. But he always gives out too much information! So, for each problem, write just the information you need to answer the question. Then solve the problem.

Read the whole problem once. Then read it again and circle the information you need. Finally, solve the problem.

1. I couldn't wait to get to the circus! We left our house at 3:03 p.m., driving at 35 miles per hour. Four of us were going—my mom, Grandpa, my sister, and me. To pass the time, we sang 8 songs. Finally we arrived at the circus at 3:54 p.m. Mom bought the tickets. They cost $3.50 each.
   How long was the drive to the circus?
   a. What information do you need to answer the question?
      time left—3:03, time arrived—3:54
   b. Solve the problem: _3:54 – 3:03 = 51   It took 51 minutes._

2. The clowns were so funny! Somehow, 42 of them crammed into a tiny car. I giggled 5 times, and I noticed 14 more people in our row laughing. I don't know how the other 8 people in the row kept a straight face! The clowns finished up their act by doing 41 somersaults and squirting each other with water from fake flowers.
   How many people were in our seating row?
   a. What information do you need to answer the question?
      _____
   b. Solve the problem: _____

3. The dancing dogs were the second act. They are my number 1 favorites! I counted 6 dogs with feathered hats. When they jumped through 12 hoops, I clapped for 4 minutes and 33 seconds! Then the 8 dogs without hats did 28 somersaults each.
   How many dogs were there in all?
   a. What information do you need to answer the question?
      _____
   b. Solve the problem: _____

Go ahead and cut out the puzzle piece. Put it in place on page 64 and you're done.

Puzzle

Here's where you glue or paste the puzzle pieces you cut out. When you put them all in place, you'll see your secret message.

Answers

Page 1

1,208 — One thousand, two hundred eight
6,410 — Six thousand, four hundred ten
3,700 — Three thousand, seven hundred
4,160 — Four thousand, one hundred sixty
3,007 — Three thousand, seven
1,028 — One thousand, twenty-eight

Page 2

A. Answer already shown
B. House number: 230,704
   Deliver to: Mel T. Plication
C. House number: 23,074
   Deliver to: Cal Q. Later
D. House number: 704,208
   Deliver to: Dee Nominator

Page 3

1. Second, first, third
2. Second, third, first
3. Second, first, third
   Bonus: Tammy won the Turtle Triathlon.

Page 4

1. (84) Cheetah
2. (357) African Elephant
3. (4,026) Ostrich
4. (194) Reticulated python
5. (7,020) Chimpanzee
6. (2,818) Koala

Page 5

1. 20, 25, 30, 35, 40, 45, 50
   Diana
2. 14, 16, 18, 20, 22, 24, 26, 28, 30, 32, 34
   Mi Won
3. 30, 40, 50
   Paul

Page 6

Lasso: $10   **1.** Spurs
Hat: $30   **2.** Lasso
Toy: $300   **3.** Boots
Spurs: $400   **4.** Hat
Boots: $200   **5.** Toy

Page 7

Answers will vary.

Page 8

$2,021 - 1,103 = 918$ $1,103 - 79 = 1,024$
$2,021 - 912 = 1,109$ $912 - 824 = 88$
$2,021 - 824 = 1,197$ $912 - 556 = 356$
$2,021 - 556 = 1,465$ $912 - 79 = 833$
$2,021 - 79 = 1,942$ $824 - 556 = 268$
$1,103 - 912 = 191$ $824 - 79 = 745$
$1,103 - 824 = 279$ $556 - 79 = 477$
$1,103 - 556 = 547$

Page 9

6, 8, 2, 6, 8, 6, 2, 9

Page 10

Frieda: 189; 140; 357
Floyd: 288; 1,722; 3,510
Florence: 2,496; 1,260; 531

Page 11

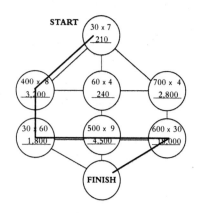

Page 12

Wilbur's score is a 70.
A. Correct.
B. Incorrect. Answer should be 32.
C. Correct.
D. Correct.
E. Correct.
F. Incorrect. Answer should be 57.
G. Correct.
H. Correct.
I. Correct.
J. Incorrect. Answer should be 65.

Page 13

Answers will vary.

Page 14

B. Florida
C. Vermont
D. Texas
E. California
F. South Carolina
G. Mississippi

Page 15

1. $4.87   3. $4.09
2. $4.35   4. $1.29

Page 16

6:20
8:07
11:34
1:45
3:11
5:52

Page 17

Pen A: 50 feet
Pen B: 48 feet
Pen C: 64 feet
Pen D: 90 feet

Page 18

Cake A: 140 square inches
Cake B: 36 square inches
Cake C: 32 square inches
Cake D: 121 square inches
Cake E: 117 square inches
Cake F: 195 square inches

Page 19

Stack A: 27 cubic units
Stack B: 64 cubic units
Stack C: 125 cubic units
Stack D: 216 cubic units

Page 20

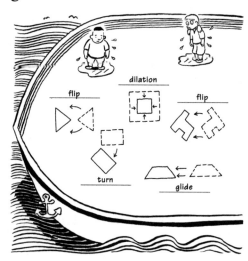

Page 21

Fish B: Minnows
Fish C: Worms
Fish D: Worms
Fish E: Minnows
Fish F: Minnows
Fish G: Worms
Fish H: Minnows

Page 22

2. $\frac{3}{4}$ 5. $\frac{3}{8}$

3. $\frac{2}{5}$ 6. $\frac{7}{8}$

4. $\frac{1}{2}$

Page 23

Answers will vary.

Page 24

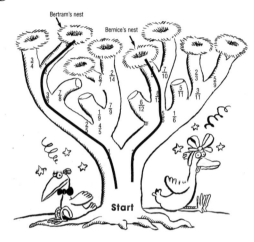

Page 25

1b. $\frac{2}{9}$ 4a. $\frac{1}{10}$

2a. $\frac{6}{7}$ b. $\frac{2}{10}$ or $\frac{1}{5}$

b. $\frac{1}{7}$ c. $\frac{3}{10}$

3a. $\frac{12}{15}$ or $\frac{4}{5}$ d. $\frac{4}{10}$ or $\frac{2}{5}$

b. $\frac{3}{15}$ or $\frac{1}{5}$ e. no

Page 26

B. Oba-chan and Oji-chan
C. Jaja and Jaja
D. Saba and Safta
E. Abuelita and Abuelito
F. Nonna and Nonno
G. Nana-ji and Nani-ji
H. Ya-ya and Pa-pu
I. Popo and Gong-gong

Page 27

B. rabbit
C. sheep
D. quail
E. tiger
F. eel
G. kangaroo
H. mackerel

Page 28

1. 35 gray tennis balls
2. 50 tennis balls in all
3. b
4. c
5. a
6. c

Page 29

2. 2 kids
3. 5 erasers
4. 10 flowers
5. 7 dogs

Page 30

2. Problem: 20 + 20
   About 40 tapes
3. Problem: 70 + 50
   About 120 balloons
4. Problem: 90 − 10
   About 80 cans
5. Problem: 80 − 20
   About 60 bags

Page 31

1. $\frac{1}{4}$ of the hats
2. $\frac{2}{5}$ of the barn
3. $\frac{1}{4}$ of the distance

Page 32

1. $4.23   3. $11.58
2. $4.25   4. No, $0.14

Page 33
A. 20   **C.** 16
B. 24   **D.** 30

Page 34
B. 6⑧3,739,251

C. ⑤27,149,003

D. 3⓪1,564,299

E. 3④,366,502

F. ⑦00,628,943

G. ⓪61,030,825

H. 38⑨,402,633

I. ④1,903,014

285,047,194

Page 35
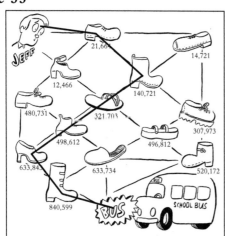

Page 36
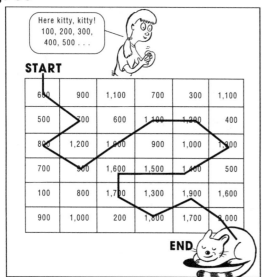

Page 37
Riddle answer: A cow eats lunch in the "CALF-ETERIA"!

Page 38
Across:	Down:
A. 41,914	**B.** 464
E. 78,487	**C.** 32,723
G. 98,289	**D.** 55,955
I. 26,062	**F.** 828
	H. 272

Page 39

26 × 32 = 832	832	64 × 13 = 832
12 × 11 = 132	52 × 16 = 832	81 × 44 = 3564
132 × 27 = 3564	3564	66 × 54 = 3564

Page 40

896 × 26 = 23296	494 × 32 = 15808	26 × 19 = 494
23,296	448 × 52 = 23296	15,808
224 × 104 = 23296	247 × 64 = 15808	988 × 16 = 15808

Page 41

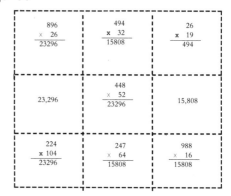

6,912	÷	72	=	96
÷		÷		÷
96	÷	12	=	8
=		=		=
72	÷	6	=	12

6,912	÷	72	=	112
÷		÷		÷
96	÷	12	=	7
=		=		=
64	÷	4	=	16

Page 42

2. Problem using rounded numbers:
   700 ÷ 50 = 14
   Each fish will get about 14 cans.
3. Original problem: 917 ÷ 88
   Problem using rounded numbers:
   900 ÷ 90 = 10
   Each fish will get about 10 cans.
4. Original problem: 1,389 ÷ 72
   Problem using rounded numbers:
   1,400 ÷ 70 = 20
   Each fish will get about 20 cans.

Page 43

2c. 18 × 45 = 810
    875 − 810 = 65
d. 875 ÷ 45 = about 19
3c. 10 × 21 = 210
    214 − 210 = 4
d. No adjustment is needed.
   214 ÷ 21 = about 10

Page 44

B. $8.00; Fiji Islands
C. $6.84; Alaska
D. $48.23; 16th century Mexico
E. $56.10; Ancient China
F. $38.70; Canada

Page 45

1. 1 hour, 30 minutes
2. 2 hours, 15 minutes
3. 2 hours, 9 minutes
4. 3 hours, 30 minutes
5. 4 hours, 18 minutes

Page 46

2. salt and pepper
3. water
4. a sandwich with lettuce, tomato, onion, and mayonnaise
5. crackers
6. an English muffin

Pages 47–48

Riddle answer: ON A RHOM-BUS!

Page 49

1. Perpendicular
2. Parallel
3.   4.

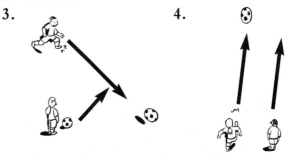

Page 50

2. Rhinoceroses
3. Hounds
4. Cats
5. Crocodiles
6. Crickets

Page 51

There are 11 circles. The pizza and one pie have diameters. One pie and the Wheel of Fortune have radii.

Page 52

Make the recipe bigger:

Sunflower seeds: $\frac{3}{6}$ cup (or $\frac{1}{2}$ cup)

Raisins: $\frac{3}{4}$ cup

Peanuts: $\frac{3}{3}$ cup (or 1 cup)

Granola: $\frac{3}{2}$ cup (or $1\frac{1}{2}$ cups)

M & Ms: $\frac{3}{3}$ cup (or 1 cup)

Make the recipe smaller:

Sunflower seeds: $\frac{1}{6}$ cup

Raisins: $\frac{1}{4}$ cup

Peanuts: $\frac{1}{3}$ cup

Granola: $\frac{1}{2}$ cup

M & Ms: $\frac{1}{3}$ cup

Page 53

2. $2\frac{6}{8}$ cherry pies (or $2\frac{3}{4}$)

3. $1\frac{3}{8}$ blueberry pies

4. $5\frac{4}{8}$ strawberry pies (or $5\frac{1}{2}$)

5. $2\frac{2}{8}$ pumpkin pies (or $2\frac{1}{4}$)

Bonus: $1\frac{3}{8}$ blueberry, $2\frac{2}{8}$ pumpkin, $2\frac{6}{8}$ cherry, $3\frac{3}{8}$ apple, $5\frac{4}{8}$ strawberry

Page 54

Rae & Ted, .4; John & Paula, .47; Viola & Stan, .37; Rob & Laura, .7;

In order from least to greatest:

1. .37; Viola and Stan
2. .4; Rae and Ted
3. .47; John and Paula
4. .7; Robert and Laura
5. .73; Babs and Doug

Page 55

Riddle answer: A HEADACHE

Page 56

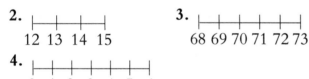

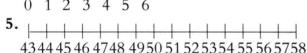

Page 57

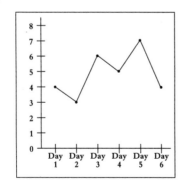

Page 58

Spinner B: FAIR
Spinner C: UNFAIR
Spinner D: FAIR
Spinner E: UNFAIR
Spinner F: FAIR

Page 59

1. Answers will vary; 5 is the most reasonable answer.
2. Answers will vary.
3. Answers will vary; 10 is the most reasonable answer.
4. Answers will vary.
5. Answers will vary.
6. Answers will vary.

Page 60

Answers will vary.

Page 61

Answers will vary.

Page 62

Riddle answer: To a MOO-SEUM!

Page 63

2a. 14 people laughing; 8 people not laughing

b. 14 + 8 = 22, There were 22 people in the seating row.

3a. 6 dogs with hats; 8 dogs without hats

b. 6 + 8 = 14, There were 14 dogs in all.

How Do You Foster Your Child's Interest in Learning?

In preparing this series, we surveyed scores of parents on this key question:

- "Even though I always buy my children books, we still continue to borrow books from the library because they have access to a better variety of books that interest them."

- "I've never forced reading on my children. My oldest son had difficulty learning to read, and the struggle made him hate it. The thing that worked was to have him focus on reading sports books that interested him. Now he avidly reads the sports section of newspapers, sports-related magazines, and sports-related nonfiction books."

- "I model good reading habits for my children by reading and belonging to a book group."

- "I put books and magazines in every bedroom and bathroom and in our living room so that my daughter and I stay in the habit of reading."

- "Talk about the characters and discuss the stories that you've just read together."

- "We do many things together as a family. We give a lot of praise and positive feedback."

- "No Nintendo! And no TV in the morning or until homework is done."

- "When her home workbooks are completed, we share them with her classroom teacher."

- "The most important thing we do is not give an immediate answer to homework questions. We try to use books, the computer, and other resources to discover the answers and information together."

- "Our seventh grader wasn't interested in reading his science book and doing science homework. Finally, my husband found out that he didn't understand what he was reading. We started reading the science book with him every day, and now he is very much interested in science."

- "We make homework low key, but non-negotiable—it's something that must get done."
- "We have a membership to a local museum that we all like to visit."
- "We like to expose our seventh-grade son to other people's lives and ideas, so we take him places."
- "I put my children in the environment of what I'd like them to learn so they experience it first-hand!"
- "Our daughter often bakes and prepares desserts with her dad."
- "We do a lot of experimenting when we cook with our children. We love to do science experiments in the kitchen together."
- "Sports are a great way for our kids to learn about life-cooperation, teamwork, leadership, goal setting..."
- "Music—music lessons, attend-ing concerts, involvement in children's symphonies and music groups—adds a great learning dimension to our kids' lives."
- "Walks are perfect learning experiences. You can really enjoy conversation and obser-vation with your children."
- "We get together as a family for regular dinners."
- "We sit down together as a family and make a family mission statement."
- "I feel that parents should take all the little questions kids have seriously and answer them truthfully."
- "We encourage our children to take art classes, and to draw, color, and create at home."
- "When grocery shopping, I ask my daughter to choose the "best buy" for the money."
- "At least twice a month we take a family nature walk. It's a great way for kids to learn about nature first hand. We take photographs to docu-ment our trips and keep them in a family album."